ISBN: 0615652050
ISBN-13: 978-0615652054

# CONTENTS

## Professional Golf Management (PGM) Interactive Flashcard Book

Comprehensive Flashcards for PGM Levels 1, 2, and 3

# LEVEL 1

**Swing Weight**

---

**Adjusting Swing Weight**

## Swing Weight

- Definition: Measure of a golf club's moment of inertia at a particular point
- Influences the overall feel and playing characteristics of a golf club
- Two primary factors that affect swing weight are the length of the shaft and mass of the clubhead
- For every 1 inch of length that is added to a driver, the swing weight will increase by 6 points
- If swing weight is too heavy, the shaft will become too flexible

---

## Adjusting Swing Weight

- Adjust swing weight by adding or removing weight from the clubhead
- To decrease swing weight, drill holes in the clubhead or hosel
- To increase swing weight, add lead tape to the lowest portion of the clubhead
- Avoid counterbalancing as a method of adjusting swing weight

**Torque**

---

**Bulge**

## Torque

- Definition: A shaft's resistance to twisting along its longitudinal axis
- Affects the angle of the clubface at impact
- Affects how the club and ball will react at impact

---

## Bulge

- Definition: Roundness of the clubface
- Compensates for off-center hits by moving the golf ball's center of gravity
- Example: A ball hit off the toe will start to the right of the target and hook back to the target as a result of bulge

**Lie**

---

**Loft**

## Lie

- Definition: Angle between the center of the golf club's shaft and a line tangent to the sole of the clubhead
- Affects the direction the clubface is pointing and how the ball leaves the clubface
- Lie angle should be fitted dynamically as the club is impacting the ball
- The shorter the club, the more upright the lie angle will be
- The longer the club, the flatter the lie angle will be
- If the lie angle is too upright, the ball will travel to the left off the clubface
- If the lie angle is too flat, the ball will travel to the right off the clubface

---

## Loft

- Definition: Angle of the clubface relative to the centerline of the golf club's hosel
- Determines the golf ball's trajectory as it leaves the clubface
- If loft is altered, the hosel set and face progression will also be changed
- Adding loft to a golf club promotes bounce
- Reducing loft from a golf club promotes dig

**Measuring the Loft of a Wood**

---

**Face Angle**

## Measuring the Loft of a Wood

- Measured at a point half the distance of the clubface height on the centerline of the clubface
- Effective loft of a wood is determined by subtracting the number of degrees the club is open from the original loft. Or it is determined by adding the number of degrees the club is closed from the original loft.

---

## Face Angle

- Definition: Angle of the clubface to the grounded sole line with the shaft perpendicular to the line of flight
- Influences the loft and direction a golf ball travels
- If the face angle is square at address, it may become closed at impact because as the shaft bows the face angle will close

**Human Variables Influencing Clubhead Speed**

---

**Maximum Clubhead Speed**

## Human Variables Influencing Clubhead Speed

- Body flexibility
- Leverage
- Neuromuscular coordination
- Physical strength
- Swing technique

---

## Maximum Clubhead Speed

Maximum clubhead speed is achieved by combining:

- Lightest overall weight
- Heaviest swing weight the golfer can reasonably assume

**Golf Club Components**

---

**Sole Inversion**

## Golf Club Components

- Clubhead
- Grip
- Shaft
- If any single component of a golf club is altered, the playing characteristics of the remaining components will also be changed

---

## Sole Inversion

- Definition: Angle of the sole of the golf club to the ground when the shaft is perpendicular to the ground and the clubface is square to the target
- 3 possible conditions are:
  - Bounce sole
  - Dig sole
  - Square sole

**Golf Ball Trajectory**

---

**Optimal Club Length**

## Golf Ball Trajectory

- Low center of gravity on the clubface will produce a high trajectory ball flight
- High center of gravity on the clubface will produce a low trajectory ball flight

---

## Optimal Club Length

- Length that produces centeredness of contact
- Club length is a determining factor of clubhead speed
- Club length should be measured at the centerline of the shaft and not from the heel of the shaft to the end of the grip

**Swing Plane**

---

**Lever System**

## Swing Plane

- Upright swing plane causes the ball to come off the clubface with a higher trajectory and a fade
- Flatter swing plane causes the ball to come off the clubface with a lower trajectory and a draw
- Flatter swing plane allows the golfer to stay better connected and time the swing more easily

---

## Lever System

- The body is a series of connected levers
- One-lever swing is swinging the left arm without cocking the wrists
- Two-lever swing is swinging the left arm and cocking the wrists
- Third lever could be created by cupping the left wrist or bending the left elbow

**Golf Ball Distance and Direction**

**Function of the Legs in the Golf Swing**

## Golf Ball Distance and Direction

- <u>Distance</u> is influenced by:
  - Angle of approach
  - Centeredness of contact
  - Clubhead speed
- <u>Direction</u> is influenced by:
  - Clubface position
  - Swing path
- Rotation is the primary motion used to generate power in the golf swing

---

## Function of the Legs in the Golf Swing

- Serves as the platform for the rotating body and swinging arms
- Places the body in a position to strike the ball with the clubface traveling in the proper direction and at the correct angle
- Maintains body balance throughout the golf swing

## Gripping the Golf Club

---

## Grip Types

## Gripping the Golf Club

Fundamentals of gripping the golf club:

- Placement: Location of the hands on the grip
- Position: Amount of hand rotation on the grip
- Pressure: How hard the grip is squeezed
- Precision: Same grip must be repeated with each swing

---

## Grip Types

- Interlocking grip is well suited for golfers with short fingers and weak grip strength
- Overlapping grip is well suited for golfers with large fingers and strong hands, wrists, and forearms
- Ten-finger grip is well suited for young golfers with small hands

**Flex Point**

---

**Casting**

## Flex Point

- Definition: Point at which the shaft of the golf club releases stored energy at impact
- Also referred to as the "bend point" or "kick point"
- Flex point can be low, mid, or high
- Flex point and ball flight are inversely related
    - Low flex point produces a high trajectory ball flight
    - High flex point produces a low trajectory ball flight

---

## Casting

- Definition: Prematurely releasing the wrist on the forward swing
- Causes the clubhead to arrive at the ball before the hands and arms

**Angle of Approach**

---

**Centrifugal Force**

## Angle of Approach

- Definition: Measure of the steepness of descent of the clubhead's forward swing
- Influences the trajectory and distance a golf ball travels
- Steeper angle of approach creates more backspin, more lift, and less distance

---

## Centrifugal Force

During the golf swing, centrifugal force has the following effects:

- Pulls the clubhead outward and downward
- Causes the arms to extend
- Makes the clubhead take a circular path

**Positional Swing Concept**

---

**Flo-Swing Concept**

## Positional Swing Concept

- Firmer = more leverage
- Well suited for:
  - Athletic golfers
  - Kinesthetic golfers
  - Long hitters
  - Low handicap golfers
- Positional swing concept and flo-swing concept are the two basic swing classifications

---

## Flo-Swing Concept

- Lighter = more centrifugal force
- Well suited for:
  - Beginners
  - Less athletic golfers
  - Short hitters
  - Visual golfers
- Flo-swing concept and positional swing concept are the two basic swing classifications

**Arc Length & Arc Width**

---

**Golf Ball Flight Laws**

## Arc Length & Arc Width

- Arc length is how far back the golf club is swung
- Arc width is the extension of the golf club away from the body
- Arc width determines distance, speed, and centeredness of contact

---

## Golf Ball Flight Laws

- Angle of approach
- Centeredness of contact
- Face
- Path
- Speed

**Principle / Law / Preference**

---

**Swing Preferences**

## Principle / Law / Preference

- Principle has direct relation to, and influence on, a law
- Law is unchangeable under any set of conditions
- Preference must directly relate to a principle in order to be valid

---

## Swing Preferences

- Preferences are the level at which golf instructors most often work
- An example of a swing preference is an inside takeaway
- There are endless possibilities of swing preferences

**Pre-Swing Principles**

---

**In-Swing Principles**

## Pre-Swing Principles

- Aim
- Grip
- Setup

---

## In-Swing Principles

- Arc length
- Arc width
- Connection
- Dynamic balance
- Impact
- Lever system
- Position
- Release
- Swing center
- Swing plane
- Timing

Kinesiology & Anatomy

---

Ligament / Tendon / Cartilage

## Kinesiology & Anatomy

- Kinesiology is the scientific study of human movement
- Anatomy is the science that studies the structure of the human body

---

## Ligament / Tendon / Cartilage

- Ligament
  - Connective tissue that limits a muscle's range of motion
  - Connects bones to other bones to form a joint
- Tendon
  - Acts as an extension of the muscle
  - Connects muscle to bone
- Cartilage
  - Flexible connective tissue
  - Found in areas of the body such as the joints between bones, the rib cage, elbows, and knees

**Muscle**

---

**Neuromuscular Coordination**

## Muscle

- Produces force and causes motion in the golf swing
- Produces power for movement in the skeletal structure
- Leg muscles maintain body balance throughout the golf swing
- Helps create and maintain posture during the golf swing

---

## Neuromuscular Coordination

- Definition: Golfer's ability to integrate his or her senses with motor function to produce accurate and skilled movement
- Using the right muscles, at the right time, with the right force

**Stretch Reflex**

---

**Dynamic Balance**

## Stretch Reflex

- Definition: Muscle contraction in response to elasticity within the muscle
- Provides automatic regulation of skeletal muscle length
- Example: During the backswing, the shoulder turn may extend beyond the rotation of the trunk
- To gain the best response from a group of muscles, the muscles need to be stretched

---

## Dynamic Balance

- Definition: Balance with movement
- Example: Transferring weight from a golfer's right side to left side during the golf swing
- Achieving dynamic balance is a key element of the proper golf swing

**Timing / Tempo / Rhythm**

---

**Golf Car Revenue**

## Timing / Tempo / Rhythm

- Timing is the sequence of movements during the golf swing
- Tempo is the rate of movement during the golf swing
- Rhythm is the flow resulting from the proper relation of parts during the golf swing

---

## Golf Car Revenue

- Golf cars are the second largest source of revenue for a golf facility behind playing fees
- Average golf car rental generates $1,900 revenue per year for a golf facility
- Average golf car rental fee is between $14 and $18 per round

## Sources of Golf Car Revenue

---

## Golf Car Revenue Calculation

## Sources of Golf Car Revenue

- Rental fees
- Trade-in value
- Trail fees from private cars

---

## Golf Car Revenue Calculation

Golf car revenue = # golf cars x # loops x $ per round

**Golf Car Expenses**

---

**Golf Car Fleet Staff**

## Golf Car Expenses

- Acquisition costs
- Car path costs
- Operating expenses
- Storage costs

---

## Golf Car Fleet Staff

Golf car fleet staff consists of:

- Attendant
- Fleet manager
- Fleet supervisor
- Maintenance supervisor
- Mechanic

**Selecting Golf Car Make and Model**

---

**Selecting Golf Car Dealer**

## Selecting Golf Car Make and Model

Consider the following:

- Appearance
- Availability
- Comfort
- Performance
- Price
- Style
- Trade-in value
- Warranty

---

## Selecting Golf Car Dealer

Consider the following:

- Delivery options
- Financing terms
- Parts and service availability
- Price
- Reputation
- Warranties

**Golf Car Fleet Manager**

---

**Factors Affecting Golf Car Fleet**

## Golf Car Fleet Manager

Responsibilities include:

- Establishing policies and procedures
- Golf car acquisition
- Maintenance
- Repair
- Storage

---

## Factors Affecting Golf Car Fleet

Golf car fleet is affected by:

- Path availability
- Terrain
- Weather
- Yardage

**Golf Car Fleet Size**

---

**Golf Car Storage**

## Golf Car Fleet Size

- Average golf car fleet size is 57 cars per facility
- 1 golf car per 8 playing members
- 1 golf car per 800 rounds played annually
- Adequate storage space for a golf car is between 70 and 75 square feet per car

---

## Golf Car Storage

Golf car storage requirements:

- Adequate space
- Available safety features (fire alarms and sprinklers)
- Location near clubhouse
- Proper ventilation

**Leasing vs. Buying a Golf Car**

---

**Golf Car Leases**

## Leasing vs. Buying a Golf Car

- Leasing
  - Better from a cash flow perspective
  - Almost always under warranty
  - No resale value
- Buying
  - Results in more equity
  - Limited warranty
  - Some resale value

---

## Golf Car Leases

- Escalating lease charges a lower cost in the first year of the lease and increases each year
- Full maintenance fixed rate lease requires the lessee to pay the same amount each month. The lessor is responsible for providing parts and services.
- Lease/purchase provides an option to purchase the golf car at the end of the lease
- Skip payment lease does not require payments during the off-season

**Golf Car Acquisition**

---

**Golf Car Fleet Record Keeping**

## Golf Car Acquisition

Loans and other funding to acquire golf cars may be provided by:

- Banks
- Commercial finance corporations
- PGA credit union
- Savings and loans

---

## Golf Car Fleet Record Keeping

Golf car fleet manager should maintain records for:

- Financing
- Maintenance
- Rotation

**Golf Car Fleet Maintenance Types**

---

**Golf Car Fleet Maintenance Program**

## Golf Car Fleet Maintenance Types

Two types of golf car maintenance:
- Preventative maintenance
- Repair

---

## Golf Car Fleet Maintenance Program

Golf car fleet maintenance program should include the following elements:
- Access to proper tools and equipment
- Adequate storage space
- Ongoing staff training
- Periodic golf car inspection
- Thorough record keeping

# Rules of Golf / Definitions / Appendices

---

## Rules of Golf: 1 through 10

## Rules of Golf / Definitions / Appendices

Rules of Golf contain:

- 34 rules
- 47 definitions
- 3 appendices

---

## Rules of Golf: 1 through 10

- Rule 1: The Game
- Rule 2: Match Play
- Rule 3: Stroke Play
- Rule 4: Clubs
- Rule 5: The Ball
- Rule 6: The Player
- Rule 7: Practice
- Rule 8: Advice; Indicating Line of Play
- Rule 9: Information as to Strokes Taken
- Rule 10: Order of Play

Rules of Golf: 11 through 20

---

Rules of Golf: 21 through 30

## Rules of Golf: 11 through 20

- Rule 11: Teeing Ground
- Rule 12: Searching for and Identifying Ball
- Rule 13: Ball Played as It Lies
- Rule 14: Striking the Ball
- Rule 15: Substituted Ball; Wrong Ball
- Rule 16: The Putting Green
- Rule 17: The Flagstick
- Rule 18: Ball at Rest Moved
- Rule 19: Ball in Motion Deflected or Stopped
- Rule 20: Lifting, Dropping and Placing; Playing from Wrong Place

---

## Rules of Golf: 21 through 30

- Rule 21: Cleaning Ball
- Rule 22: Ball Assisting or Interfering with Play
- Rule 23: Loose Impediments
- Rule 24: Obstructions
- Rule 25: Abnormal Ground Conditions, Embedded Ball and Wrong Putting Green
- Rule 26: Water Hazards (Including Lateral Water Hazards)
- Rule 27: Ball Lost or Out of Bounds; Provisional Ball
- Rule 28: Ball Unplayable
- Rule 29: Threesomes and Foursomes
- Rule 30: Three-ball, Best-Ball, and Four-Ball Match Play

# Rules of Golf: 31 through 34

---

# Appendices to the Rules of Golf

## Rules of Golf: 31 through 34

- Rule 31: Four-Ball Stroke Play
- Rule 32: Bogey, Par, and Stableford Competitions
- Rule 33: The Committee
- Rule 34: Disputes and Decisions

---

## Appendices to the Rules of Golf

- Appendix I: Local Rules; Conditions of the Competition
- Appendix II: Design of Clubs
- Appendix III: The Ball

**Penalty for Rule Violation**

---

**Penalty for Ethics Violation**

## Penalty for Rule Violation

- Penalty in stroke play for a rule violation is 2 strokes
- Penalty in match play for a rule violation is loss of hole
- Penalties apply unless otherwise noted

---

## Penalty for Ethics Violation

Possible penalties for a PGA ethics violation:

- Monetary fine up to $1,000
- Loss of playing privileges in sectional and national events
- Suspension or expulsion from the PGA

**Original Rules of Golf**

---

**Changes to the Rules of Golf**

## Original Rules of Golf

- Created in 1744
- 13 rules
- Originally titled "The Articles and Laws in Playing Golf"

---

## Changes to the Rules of Golf

- Changes may be made to the Rules of Golf every 4 years
- Changes may be made to the Decisions on the Rules of Golf every 2 years
- USGA Rules Committee meets twice per year to discuss proposed rule changes
- Rules Drafting Committee is responsible for developing the language for proposed rule changes

**Golf Ball Specifications**

---

**USGA and R&A**

## Golf Ball Specifications

- Golf balls shall weigh a maximum of 1.62 ounces
- Golf balls shall have a maximum diameter of 1.68 inches
- Specifications agreed upon by the USGA and R&A in 1920

---

## USGA and R&A

- United States Golf Association (USGA) was founded in 1894
- Royal and Ancient Golf Club (R&A) became the governing world authority for the Rules of Golf in 1897
- USGA and R&A have not always held the same rules at the same time

**Movable vs. Immovable Obstructions**

---

**"Through the Green"**

## Movable vs. Immovable Obstructions

- Movable obstructions
  - Moved without unreasonable effort
  - Moved without delaying play
  - Moved without damage
- Immovable obstructions
  - Takes reasonable effort to move
  - Causes delay in play to move

---

## "Through the Green"

Defined as the whole area of the golf course except:

- Teeing area of the hole being played
- Putting green of the hole being played
- All hazards on the golf course

## Loose Impediments

---

## Loose Impediment Exclusions

## Loose Impediments

Natural objects such as:

- Insects
- Stones
- Twigs
- Worms

---

## Loose Impediment Exclusions

Loose impediments exclude items that are:

- Adhering to the ball
- Embedded
- Fixed
- Growing

**Identifying Ground Under Repair**

---

**Identifying Water Hazards**

## Identifying Ground Under Repair

Ground under repair may be identified by:

- Orange stakes, or
- White lines

---

## Identifying Water Hazards

Water hazards may be identified by:

- Yellow stakes, or
- Yellow lines

**Water Hazard Relief Options**

---

**Lateral Water Hazard Relief Options**

## Water Hazard Relief Options

- Play the ball as it lies
- Play the ball as near as possible from where the ball was last played
- Drop the ball on an extended line between the flagstick and where the ball last crossed the hazard

---

## Lateral Water Hazard Relief Options

- Drop the ball at a point equidistant from where the ball last crossed the hazard, no nearer to the hole
- Drop the ball two club lengths from the point where the ball last crossed the hazard, no nearer to the hole

Handicap Systems

---

Tournament Pairing Sheet

## Handicap Systems

- Blind Bogey handicap system matches a competitor's net score to a randomly selected number between 70 and 90
- Callaway handicap system deducts a number of the worst hole scores from the combined score of the first 16 holes

---

## Tournament Pairing Sheet

Tournament pairing sheet includes:

- Event format
- Handicaps
- Tournament officials

**PGA of America**

---

**PGA Constitution**

## PGA of America

- Founded in 1916
- Mission is to promote the enjoyment and involvement of the game of golf, and to contribute to its growth by providing services to golf professionals, consumers, and the golf industry
- There are approximately 28,000 men and women PGA Professionals and PGA Apprentices

---

## PGA Constitution

- Article 1: Name and Purpose
- Article 2: Membership
- Article 3: Organization
- Article 4: Meetings
- Article 5: PGA Tour

**Bylaws & Regulations**

---

**Penalty for PGA Constitution Rule Violation**

## Bylaws & Regulations

- Bylaws outline the general philosophies, practices, and procedures of the PGA Constitution, as agreed upon by the Association
- Regulations explain the Bylaws of the PGA Constitution

---

## Penalty for PGA Constitution Rule Violation

Possible penalties for a PGA Constitution rule violation:

- Expulsion
- Probation
- Reprimand
- Suspension

**PGA Officers**

---

**PGA Board of Directors**

## PGA Officers

- President serves as the Chairman of the Board, presides at all meetings, and serves as the spokesman for the Association
- Vice president is responsible for managing all financial matters for the Association
- Secretary is responsible for managing all membership matters for the Association, and serves as the Chairperson for the Board of Control
- Honorary president is the immediate former PGA President

---

## PGA Board of Directors

PGA Board of Directors consists of:

- President
- Vice president
- Secretary
- Honorary president
- Player director
- Director from each district
- 2 independent contractors

**PGA Board of Control**

---

**Golf Facility Evaluation**

## PGA Board of Control

- Reviews membership matters
- Meets quarterly
- Includes the PGA Secretary and four individuals appointed by the PGA President, representing the four geographical areas of the United States
- Must be a past national director, sectional officer, or national officer to serve on the Board of Control

---

## Golf Facility Evaluation

Golf facilities should be evaluated on the following criteria:

- Number of members
- Number of 18-hole rounds played
- Number of lessons
- Number of bags in storage
- Number of tournaments
- Size of golf car fleet
- Merchandise sales
- Merchandise inventory levels

**PGA Recognized Golf Course**

---

**PGA Recognized Golf Range**

## PGA Recognized Golf Course

- 9-hole golf course must be at least 1,000 yards in length
- 18-hole golf course must be at least 1,500 yards in length
- Must have at least 14 acres of total course area, excluding the clubhouse, golf shop, and parking area

---

## PGA Recognized Golf Range

- Minimum of 15 tees and 150 feet of teeing area
- Depth of at least 600 feet
- PGA Professional must be available for instruction

**Director of Golf**
**Roles & Responsibilities**

---

**General Manager**
**Roles & Responsibilities**

## Director of Golf
## Roles & Responsibilities

Directs the total golf operation including:

- Golf shop
- Golf range
- Golf car fleet
- Supervision of Head Professional

---

## General Manager
## Roles & Responsibilities

- Develops annual business plan
- Implements general policies and procedures
- Maintains organizational structure
- Oversees relationship between the facility, its patrons, employees, community, government, and industry

**Head PGA Professional Roles & Responsibilities**

---

**Assistant PGA Professional Roles & Responsibilities**

## Head PGA Professional Roles & Responsibilities

Head PGA Professional is responsible for:

- Handicapping
- Hiring
- Recruiting
- Starting & tee times
- Supervising
- Training

---

## Assistant PGA Professional Roles & Responsibilities

- Bookkeeping
- Club repair
- Golf car operations
- Handicapping
- Merchandising
- Tournament operations
- Staff scheduling

**PGA Apprentice Requirements**

---

**PGA Districts & Sections**

## PGA Apprentice Requirements

- At least 18 years old
- Eligibly employed for at least 6 months
- Endorsed by a PGA member
- High school diploma or equivalency
- Pass the Playing Ability Test (PAT)
- Pay required fees

---

## PGA Districts & Sections

- 14 PGA Districts
- 41 PGA Sections
- In order to become a PGA Section, there must be at least 50 PGA Professionals within a 140 mile radius

**Rights of PGA Members**

---

**Maintaining PGA Membership Status**

## Rights of PGA Members

PGA members have the right to:

- Attend annual meetings as an observer
- Hold office
- Use the PGA name and logo
- Vote

---

## Maintaining PGA Membership Status

- Must achieve a minimum number of professional development points (PDPs) to be earned in a 3-year period, as determined by the Board of Directors
- Members who do not meet PDP requirements will be designated as Class "F" members

**PGA Teaching Triangle**

**Methods of Learning the Golf Swing**

## PGA Teaching Triangle

- Three parts of the teaching triangle are what, how, and when
    - What the instructor selects to teach
    - How the instructor communicates with students
    - When the instructor introduces specific elements of the golf swing

---

## Methods of Learning the Golf Swing

- Verbal
- Visual
- Kinesthetic (recommended form)

**A-B-C Golf Swing Model**

---

**Golf Swing Learning Model**

## A-B-C Golf Swing Model

- Technique used to keep golf instruction simple
- Teach the golf swing in three steps
    1. Preparing to swing
    2. Top of swing
    3. Finish of swing

---

## Golf Swing Learning Model

Four parts of the golf swing learning model:

1. Input
2. Integration
3. Output
4. Feedback

**Instructor Feedback**

---

**Improving Student Motivation**

## Instructor Feedback

Three functions of a golf instructor providing feedback to a student:

- Fix an error
- Provide motivation
- Serve as reinforcement

---

## Improving Student Motivation

Techniques to improve student motivation:

- Praise
- Recognition
- Reward

**Evaluating Teaching Aids**

---

**Establishing Teaching Goals**

## Evaluating Teaching Aids

- Is the teaching aid helpful?
- Is it cost effective?
- Is it easy to set up?
- Is it easy to use?
- Is it reliable?
- Is it well made?

---

## Establishing Teaching Goals

- Instructor and student should establish goals together
- Goals should be challenging but attainable
- Goals should be specific
- Goals should progress from short-term to long-term

## Critical Error & Master Key

## Teaching Drills

## Critical Error & Master Key

- "Critical error" is a single error the student makes that causes additional errors to be made
- The "master key" is to fix the critical error because it will help fix other errors as well

---

## Teaching Drills

Teaching drills provide the following benefits:

- Cure specific swing errors
- Isolate parts of the swing
- Promote feel
- Reinforce positive habits
- Teach correct swing position

## Elements of an Employment Contract

---

## Employment Contract Clauses

## Elements of an Employment Contract

- Compensation
- Duties and responsibilities of the employer
- Duties and responsibilities of the position
- Policies on time off
- Termination clause
- Term of the contract

---

## Employment Contract Clauses

- Arbitration clause specifies that any controversy or claim arising from the contract will be subject to arbitration
- Evergreen clause provides an automatic annual extension of the employment contract if neither party notifies the other that they wish to terminate the agreement
- Inflation adjustment provision provides an annual cost of living increase correlated with the Consumer Price Index
- Merger clause explains what will happen to a golf professional if his or her golf facility is bought or merged with another
- Non-compete clause specifies that an employee may not work at a competing facility for a specified period of time following separation from service

**Arbitration**

---

**Deferred Compensation**

## Arbitration

- May be voluntary or mandatory
- May be binding or non-binding
- Less expensive than litigation
- Less time consuming than litigation
- Employment contract may specify that any controversy or claim arising from the contract will be subject to arbitration

---

## Deferred Compensation

- Definition: Arrangement in which a portion of a golf professional's income is paid out at a date after which the income is actually earned
- Examples:
    - Pensions
    - Retirement plans
    - Stock options

**COBRA**

---

**Fringe Benefits**

## COBRA

- Consolidated Omnibus Budget Reconciliation Act (COBRA)
- Employers must provide former employees and their families with the opportunity to purchase heath care coverage that is identical to the coverage they received when they were employed
- Applies to employers with 20 or more employees
- Coverage is limited to 18 months for employees
- Coverage is limited to 36 months for dependents

---

## Fringe Benefits

Fringe benefits provided to a golf professional may include:

- Health insurance
- Life insurance
- On-duty meals
- Personal use of golf facility
- Retirement plan
- Vacation time

**Child Labor Rules**

---

**Federal Employment Laws**

## Child Labor Rules

- 14- and 15-year-old minors may work no more than 3 hours on a school day, and 8 hours on a non-school day
- 14- and 15-year-old minors may work no more than 18 hours per week when school is in session, and 40 hours per week when school is not in session
- 14- and 15-year-old minors may not work before 7:00 am or after 7:00 pm

---

## Federal Employment Laws

- Age Discrimination in Employment Act (ADEA) prohibits employers from discriminating against workers older than age 40
- Americans with Disabilities Act (ADA) prohibits employers from discriminating against a qualified disabled worker if the worker is able to perform all of the duties required for the job
- Civil Rights Act of 1964 states that it is illegal for a company to not hire an applicant because of the applicant's gender, race, or religion

**Federal Employment Laws**

---

**Federal Employment Laws**

## Federal Employment Laws

- Equal Pay Act of 1963 requires equal pay for equal work, regardless of sex
- Fair Credit Reporting Act requires an employer to inform the applicant in writing if they plan to conduct a background check
- Fair Labor Standards Act of 1938 set standards for minimum wage, overtime pay, child labor, and record keeping
- Garnishment Laws require a court order to have an employer withhold money from an employee's wage for payment of a debt to a third party. Applies to child support, bankruptcy, and unpaid taxes.

---

## Federal Employment Laws

- Immigration Reform and Control Act (IRCA) requires employers to verify the identity and work status of each new employee the company hires
- Occupational Safety and Health Act (OSHA) requires employers to provide employees with a safe and healthy work environment
- Veterans Rights and Military Service Act requires companies to rehire employees who were called to, or volunteered for, military service

## PGA Employment Services

---

## Preparing for a Job Interview

## PGA Employment Services

- Career Net
- Career Links
- Career Chips

---

## Preparing for a Job Interview

- Research the facility
- Research the interviewer
- Review the facility's annual report
- Review the facility's brochure
- Provide a cover letter and résumé to each interviewer

**Types of Résumés**

---

**Include / Exclude From Résumé**

## Types of Résumés

- Functional
- Targeted
- Chronological (most common)

---

## Include / Exclude From Résumé

- Include on résumé:
  - Community service
  - Educational experience
  - Extracurricular activities
  - Military service
  - Objective
  - Professional affiliations
- Exclude on résumé:
  - Religious affiliations
  - Social affiliations

## Networking Etiquette

## Networking Etiquette

- Introduce yourself
- Request information about the golf facility
- Ask for names of decision makers
- Thank others for their time

# LEVEL 2

**Golf Facility Mission Statement**

---

**SWOT Analysis**

## Golf Facility Mission Statement

- Guides and motivates employees
- Keeps management focused
- Includes goals regarding a golf facility's:
    - Image
    - Profitability
    - Quality of service

---

## SWOT Analysis

- Definition: Strategic business planning tool used to evaluate a company's strengths, weaknesses, opportunities, and threats
- Strengths and weaknesses evaluate internal factors
- Opportunities and threats evaluate external factors

## Golf Facility Items to Forecast

---

## Performance Formulas

## Golf Facility Items to Forecast

- Cost of goods sold
- Expenses
- Gross margin
- Number of rounds played
- Profit
- Revenue

---

## Performance Formulas

- COGS % = cost of goods sold / total retail sales
- Gross margin % = (revenue – cost of goods sold) / revenue
- Net total value = original cost – accumulated depreciation
- Profit = revenue – (cost of goods sold + expenses)

**Internal Factors Affecting Economic Forecast**

---

**External Factors Affecting Economic Forecast**

## Internal Factors Affecting Economic Forecast

- Customer service
- Facility characteristics
- Financial resources
- Staff resources

---

## External Factors Affecting Economic Forecast

- Golf industry trends
- National economic trends
- Regulatory trends
- Weather

**Performance Analysis**

---

**Linear Trend Analysis**

## Performance Analysis

Two types of performance analysis:

- Linear trend analysis
- Base-year analysis

---

## Linear Trend Analysis

- Formula: (later year sales – previous year sales) / previous year sales = % change
- Used to calculate the percentage change from year to year for line items such as number of rounds played, revenue, and expenses
- Use when there is over 5 years of historical data to compare, and the data is being compared horizontally

## Base-Year Analysis

---

## Depreciation / Amortization / Depletion

## Base-Year Analysis

- Formula: (year's sales you want to compare / base year sales) x 100 = % change from base year
- Use if Head Professional wants to track improved golf shop sales relative to the year he was hired

---

## Depreciation / Amortization / Depletion

- Depreciation is the process by which the tax basis of a tangible asset is recovered
- Amortization is the process by which the tax basis of an intangible asset is recovered
- Depletion is the process by which the tax basis of natural resources is recovered

**Budgeting Process**

---

**Types of Budgets**

## Budgeting Process

1. Estimate all income and sources of income
2. Review all fixed and discretionary expenses
3. Determine how much will be saved or invested

---

## Types of Budgets

- Capital budget includes the cost of financing long-term projects, such as renovations to a golf course and its buildings
- Cash flow budget projects how much cash a golf facility will have in its bank account at the end of the budget period
- Operational budget provides an overview of a golf facility's day-to-day income and expenses

**Elements of Effective Staffing**

---

**Policies & Procedures**

## Elements of Effective Staffing

- Determine staff needs
- Determine staff skills
- Establish performance standards
- Use organizational charts to establish reporting relationships

---

## Policies & Procedures

- Policies are rules or principles provided by management that outline a specific course of action
- Procedures are step-by-step instructions which must be executed in a specific manner to complete a task

Procedure Writing Guidelines

---

Customer Service

## Procedure Writing Guidelines

- Use clear and concise language
- Use simple, short words and sentences
- Start each sentence with a verb
- Provide examples
- Number each step

---

## Customer Service

Key elements to successful customer service:
- Resources
- Staffing
- Systems

**Understanding Customer Needs**

---

**"Moment of Truth"**

## Understanding Customer Needs

To understand customer needs, the golf professional should:

- Conduct a survey
- Host a focus group
- Review the complaint log
- Evaluate returned merchandise
- Ask customers directly

---

## "Moment of Truth"

- Definition: Any experience customers have with a business that provides them with an opportunity to evaluate the quality of their products and services
- Example: When guests arrive at a golf club to find dirty towels lying in the locker room they are experiencing a "moment of truth"

**Dissatisfied Customers**

---

**Task-Relationship Connection**

## Dissatisfied Customers

- 1 unhappy customer will tell 9 others
- 13% of dissatisfied customers will tell at least 20 people
- 90% of dissatisfied customers will not return to a golf facility
- 96% of dissatisfied customers will not complain directly

---

## Task-Relationship Connection

- Task component
    - Identifies what the golf professional is trying to achieve
    - Golf professional should ask himself: "How does the way I handle this task build or detract from the relationship?"
- Relationship component
    - Identifies the quality of the interaction between the golf professional and the customer
    - Golf professional should ask himself: "How does the way I handle the relationship with the customer support or limit completing the task?"

**GEODE Model**

---

**GEODE Model Examples**

## GEODE Model

GEODE model for handling day-to-day customer relations:

- Greet
- Enquire
- Offer
- Deliver
- Evaluate

---

## GEODE Model Examples

- Greet: Golf professional frames the customer interaction as problem-solving rather than confrontational
- Enquire: Golf professional shows understanding and empathy, and confirms the customer's needs by restating the customer's concerns and checking for agreement
- Offer: Golf professional proposes a solution and describes its limitations
- Deliver: Golf professional determines specific arrangements and provides a meaningful extra touch
- Evaluate: Golf professional asks the customer for feedback

**Interpersonal Skills**

**Interpersonal Skill Examples**

## Interpersonal Skills

- Act with integrity
- Encourage open expression
- Invite and give specific feedback
- Provide a compelling rationale
- Reframe difficult situations
- Show understanding
- State your purpose clearly

---

## Interpersonal Skill Examples

- Acting with integrity demonstrates dependability and trustworthiness
- Encouraging open expression evokes participation through active involvement
- Inviting and giving specific feedback provides opportunity to clarify misunderstandings and change behavior
- Providing a compelling rationale bridges gap between what golf professional offers and what customer wants
- Reframing difficult situations finds positive intent that may be hidden in a negative response
- Showing understanding reduces defensiveness by establishing empathy
- Stating your purpose clearly establishes direction and alignment

## Interaction Strategies

---

## Interaction Strategy Examples

## Interaction Strategies

- Convincing strategy
- Directing strategy
- Involving strategy
- Supporting strategy

---

## Interaction Strategy Examples

- Convincing helps others see the value of adopting your solution
- Directing involves telling others explicitly what to do
- Involving invites others to join with your solution
- Supporting helps others find their own unique problem solving solution

**When to Use Interaction Strategies**

---

**Golf Instructor Traits**

## When to Use Interaction Strategies

- Convincing strategy should be used by a manager if an employee is resistant and inexperienced
- Directing strategy should be used by a manager if an employee is enthusiastic and inexperienced
- Involving strategy should be used by a manager if an employee is resistant and experienced
- Supporting strategy should be used by a manager if an employee is enthusiastic and experienced

---

## Golf Instructor Traits

Factors that make an exceptional golf instructor include:

- Communication skills
- Credibility
- Energy
- Enthusiasm
- Golf knowledge
- Motivation

**Maximum Number of Lessons per Day**

---

**Methods of Acquiring Golf Knowledge**

## Maximum Number of Lessons per Day

- Varies according to a golf instructor's physical strength and mental stamina
- Suggested maximum number of lessons per day:
  - 10 half-hour lessons, or
  - 6 one-hour lessons

---

## Methods of Acquiring Golf Knowledge

- Books
- Clinics
- Demonstrations
- Lessons
- Observing successful players
- Personal playing
- Seminars
- Studying videotape

**Club Fitting Steps**

---

**Golf Club Evaluation**

## Club Fitting Steps

4. Interview the golfer regarding his swing tendencies and physical limitations
5. Evaluate the golfer's current clubs
6. Observe the golfer hitting balls
7. Provide club fitting recommendation

---

## Golf Club Evaluation

Three elements to evaluate whether a golf club will improve a player's performance:

- Design
- Fit
- Quality

**Steel Shafts**

---

**Graphite Shafts**

## Steel Shafts

- Flex characteristics are controlled by wall thickness
- Thinner steel shaft
  - Lighter
  - More flexible
  - More torque
- Thicker steel shaft
  - Heavier
  - Stiffer
  - Less torque

---

## Graphite Shafts

- Transmit fewer vibrations up the shaft to golfer's hands than steel shafts
- Stiffness, flex points, and torque are controlled by:
  - Amount of fiber
  - Fiber's tensile strength
  - Pattern in which the fibers are applied

**Conforming Golf Ball**

---

**Factors Affecting Golf Ball Distance**

## Conforming Golf Ball

Conforming golf balls must pass a test on:

- Initial velocity
- Overall distance
- Size
- Symmetry of design pattern
- Weight

---

## Factors Affecting Golf Ball Distance

- Dimple design
- Material of the cover and core
- Size
- Weight

**Factors Affecting Golf Ball Performance**

---

**Centeredness of Contact**

## Factors Affecting Golf Ball Performance

- Aerodynamics
- Compression
- Durability
- Material

---

## Centeredness of Contact

Centeredness of contact is influenced by:

- Clubhead path
- Clubhead speed
- Clubface angle
- Clubface impact location

**Fundamentals of Hitting an Iron Shot**

---

**Superintendent**
**Roles & Responsibilities**

## Fundamentals of Hitting an Iron Shot

- Clubhead should strike the ball with a descending arc
- Clubhead's center of gravity at impact should be equal to, or lower than, the golf ball's center of gravity

---

## Superintendent Roles & Responsibilities

- Responsible for managing the golf course, grounds surrounding the golf course, practice putting greens, golf range, parking area, and entrance road
- Hires, trains, evaluates, and manages the year-round and seasonal maintenance staff
- Oversees the turfgrass management program
- Achieves compliance with the EPA (Environmental Protection Agency) and OSHA (Occupational Safety and Health Administration)

**Essential Nutrients for Turfgrass Survival**

---

**Zones of Turfgrass Adaptation**

## Essential Nutrients for Turfgrass Survival

- 15 essential nutrients for turfgrass survival occur naturally in sufficient quantities in the air
- 3 essential nutrients may be supplemented through fertilizers
  - Nitrogen
  - Phosphorus
  - Potassium

---

## Zones of Turfgrass Adaptation

- Cool season grass
- Warm season grass
- Transition zone

**Characteristics of Cool Season Grass**

---

**Characteristics of Warm Season Grass**

## Characteristics of Cool Season Grass

- Thrive in temperatures between 60 and 75 degrees
- Grass stays green all year in areas with mild winters
- Grass becomes dormant and turns brown in areas that receive snow

---

## Characteristics of Warm Season Grass

- Thrive in temperatures between 80 and 95 degrees
- Grass becomes dormant and turns brown if the temperature drops below 50 degrees
- Overseeding may be used to maintain green grass all year

**Northern Climate Grass**

---

**Southern Climate Grass**

## Northern Climate Grass

- Bentgrass
- Bluegrass
- Fescue
- Ryegrass

---

## Southern Climate Grass

- Bermudagrass
- Buffalograss
- Zoysiagrass

**Function of a Plant's Roots and Shoots**

---

**Removing a Plant's Shoot**

## Function of a Plant's Roots and Shoots

- Roots
  - Absorb water and nutrients for the plan
- Shoots
  - Need sunlight to produce food for the plant
  - Grasses are able to regenerate their shoots if they're not cut too closely to their growing points
  - In plants, the growing point is at the tip of the shoot
  - In grass, the growing point is at the base of the shoot

---

## Removing a Plant's Shoot

- Reduces a plant's resistance to the invasion of disease
- Reduces a plant's ability to absorb water and nutrients
- Reduces a plant's ability to make its own food

**Types of Soil**

---

**Soil Content**

## Types of Soil

- Soil is classified by the size of its particles
- Sandy soil is composed of large particles that allow water and nutrients to pass through so quickly that they're not readily available for the plant
- Clay soil tends to retain water and leaves little room for oxygen
- Loam soil creates a stable growing environment for the plant by providing a balance between drainage and retention

---

## Soil Content

Soil is approximately:

- 25% air
- 25% water
- 50% solid

**Soil pH**

---

**Soil Compaction**

# Soil pH

- Soil pH measures soil acidity and alkalinity
- A measure of 0 is highly acidic, and a measure of 14 is highly alkaline
- Turfgrass grows best in soil that is slightly acidic (pH of 6.0 to 6.5)
- Clay soil tends to be acidic
- Sandy soil tends to be alkaline
- Lime may be added to soil to raise its pH level
- Sulfur may be added to soil to lower its pH level

---

# Soil Compaction

- Occurs when the weight of heavy machinery compresses soil and causes a loss of pore space
- May also occur due to lack of water in the soil

**Fertilizer**

---

**Syringing**

## Fertilizer

Bag of fertilizer that reads 10-6-4 contains:

- 10% nitrogen
- 6% phosphorus
- 4% potassium

---

## Syringing

- Definition: Technique used to cool turfgrass through a light application of water to the grass surface
- Should be applied at the first sign of wilt
- During periods of excessive heat, syringing may be applied up to 3 times daily

**Aeration**

---

**Topdressing**

## Aeration

- Definition: Removing 3 to 4 inches of ground soil to restore the passageways that facilitate the flow of water, nutrients, and air to the plant
- Stimulates the growth of new roots by increasing air supply to the roots
- Allows water and nutrients to penetrate into the root zone

---

## Topdressing

- Definition: Placing a layer of soil over the putting surface to smooth and decrease surface irregularities
- Performed immediately after aerating
- Slowly alters soil content over time

**Overseeding**

---

**Mowing**

## Overseeding

- Definition: Planting cool season grass over warm season grass
- Provides green playing surface during winter months
- Primarily used in southern areas of the country

---

## Mowing

- Longer grass tends to be healthier than shorter grass
- Shorter heights are stressful for all types of grass
- Grasses that best tolerate shorter mowing heights are bermudagrass and bentgrass
- Shorter mowing heights create a turfgrass environment that requires more active maintenance

**Mowing Heights**

---

**Mowing Frequency**

## Mowing Heights

- Suggested mowing height for greens is 1/8" to 1/4"
- Suggested mowing height for tees is 3/8" to 1"
- Suggested mowing height for fairways is 1/2" to 1¼"
- Suggested mowing height for rough is 2" or higher

---

## Mowing Frequency

- Greens can be mowed once or twice per day depending on golf course conditions
- Tees and fairways should be mowed 2 to 4 times per week depending on golf course conditions
- Rough should be mowed weekly, monthly, or seasonally

**Pest Categories**

---

**Pest Control**

## Pest Categories

Three broad categories of pests found on a golf course:

- Diseases
- Insects
- Weeds

---

## Pest Control

- Apply fungicide to eliminate diseases
- Apply herbicide to eliminate weeds
- Apply insecticide to eliminate insects

**Integrated Pest Management (IPM)**

---

**Insect Prevention**

## Integrated Pest Management (IPM)

- Places an emphasis on pest prevention rather than eradication
- Superintendent should take appropriate but minimum action at first
- Superintendent should only take additional action if necessary to eradicate pests

---

## Insect Prevention

- Apply adequate fertilizer
- Keep thatch at a minimum
- Keep turfgrass free of weeds
- Use insecticide at first sign of insects

**Surface Insects**

---

**Subsurface Insects**

## Surface Insects

- Surface insects found on a golf course:
    - Armyworms
    - Beetles
    - Chinch bugs
    - Cutworms
    - Fruit flies
    - Sod webworms
    - Vegetable weevils
- Turf that is beginning to die along curbs or sidewalks, even with adequate watering, is an indication that surface insects may be present

---

## Subsurface Insects

- Subsurface insects found on a golf course:
    - Bermuda grass mites
    - Billbug grubs
    - Centipedes
    - Mole crickets
    - Nematodes
    - White grubs
- Overall thinning of turf is a warning sign that subsurface insects may be present

**Thatch**

---

**Turfgrass Disease**

## Thatch

- Definition: Layer of organic matter that accumulates just below the grass blades and above the soil surface
- Thick thatch may be harmful and should be removed (dethatched)
- Excess thatch prevents water, nutrients, fertilizers, and insecticides from penetrating into the soil and plant roots

---

## Turfgrass Disease

- Turfgrass disease is primarily a result of fungus
- Use fungicide at the first sign of turfgrass disease
- Turfgrass diseases include:
    - Brown patch
    - Dollar spot
    - Fairy ring
    - Grease spot (Pythium blight)

**Plants & Weeds**

---

**Phases of Golf Course Design**

## Plants & Weeds

- Plants are classified by their lifecycle and plant structure
- A weed is defined as a plant in an undesired location
- Use herbicide to kill unwanted plants on a golf course
- Weeds grow due to soil compaction, poor drainage, excess watering, weak turfgrass, and short mowing heights

---

## Phases of Golf Course Design

- Phase I: Site analysis
- Phase II: Design
- Phase III: Development
- Phase IV: Grow-in
- Phase V: Maintenance

**Golf Course Design Schedule**

---

**Golf Course Design Core Team**

## Golf Course Design Schedule

- Phase I (site analysis) takes 4 to 6 months to complete
- Phase II (design takes 6 to 18 months to complete
- Phase III (development) takes 12 to 18 months to complete
- Phase IV (grow-in) takes 3 to 10 months to complete
- Phase V (maintenance) is ongoing and never complete

---

## Golf Course Design Core Team

- Architect
- Contractor
- Superintendent

**Phase I: Site Analysis**

---

**Hired During Phase I: Site Analysis**

## Phase I: Site Analysis

Golf course design core team should evaluate and review the following:

- Available resources
- Available utilities
- Compatibility
- Environmental conditions
- Land
- Legal requirements
- Political landscape

---

## Hired During Phase I: Site Analysis

- Archaeologists
- Environmentalists
- Financial advisors
- Hydrologists
- Land planners
- Legal counsel

**Phase II: Design**

---

**Hired During Phase II: Design**

## Phase II: Design

Design phase is completed in the following order:

1. Create base map
2. Create routing plan
3. Create concept plan
4. Create construction plan

---

## Hired During Phase II: Design

- Building architects
- Interior designers
- Landscape architects
- Publicists

**Base Map**

---

**Routing Plan**

## Base Map

- Part of the design phase (Phase II)
- Base map includes:
    - Environmental resources
    - Historical sites
    - Right-of-ways
    - Structures
    - Underground utilities

---

## Routing Plan

- Part of the design phase (Phase II)
- Also referred to as a schematic
- Steps to develop a routing plan:
    1. Identify possible locations for the clubhouse
    2. Identify a practice facility site at each potential clubhouse location

**Concept Plan**

---

**Construction Plan**

## Concept Plan

- Part of the design phase (Phase II)
- Provides a visual image of how the golf course will look once it is complete
- Displays the shape, size, and form of each golf course feature, including tees, greens, bunkers, and hazards

---

## Construction Plan

- Part of the design phase (Phase II)
- Guides the building of a golf course
- Includes specific plans for:
    - Grading
    - Irrigation
    - Landscaping
- Finishing the construction plan marks the end of the golf course design phase (Phase II), and the beginning of the development phase (Phase III)

**Phase III: Development**

---

**Hired During Phase III: Development**

## Phase III: Development

Development phase is completed in the following order:

1. Staking
2. Clearing
3. Rough grading and major drainage
4. Feature construction and minor drainage
5. Irrigation
6. Finished grading and planting preparation
7. Planting

---

## Hired During Phase III: Development

- Bricklayers
- Concrete pourers
- Heavy equipment operators
- Irrigation specialists

# Phase IV: Grow-In

---

## Irrigation System

## Phase IV: Grow-In

Install and build the following:

- Chemical storage facility
- Golf car paths
- Golf car storage area
- Parking area
- Shelters
- Signs, tee markers, and ball washers

---

## Irrigation System

Golf course irrigation system may be:

- Automatic or manual
- Single line or double line
- Electrical or hydraulic

**Surface Drainage**

---

**Subsurface Drainage**

## Surface Drainage

- Primarily a function of the land's topography
- Determined by the slope and shape of the land

---

## Subsurface Drainage

- Definition: Internal drainage of the soil
- Primarily a function of soil content
- Subsurface drainage may be created by:
    - Constructing drainage systems
    - Soil amendments
- Typically used in areas of the golf course that require the highest level of maintenance, such as tees and greens

**Modern Methods of Greens Construction**

---

**Green Design**

## Modern Methods of Greens Construction

- California Greens Construction Method
- Topsoil Greens Construction Method
- USGA Greens Construction Method

---

## Green Design

- Greens typically range from 5,000 to 8,000 square feet at PGA recognized golf courses
- There should be a 12 to 15 foot collar around the perimeter of each green where no cups should be placed
- Each green should have 12 to 20 areas for possible cup placement, with a 3 foot radius around each cup with no slope
- Greens should vary in size, shape, and contour
- Greens should hold a well-played approach shot

**Tee Area Design**

---

**Use of Hazards on a Golf Course**

## Tee Area Design

- Tee area for each hole should be at least 6,000 square feet
- Because they receive more wear, the first, tenth, and par-3 tees typically average 8,000 square feet or more
- Golfers should be able to view the entire hole from the tee area
- Contour of the tee area should direct golfers towards the intended line of play

---

## Use of Hazards on a Golf Course

- Integrate natural features when possible
- Hazards are intended to:
  - Challenge golfers
  - Direct play
  - Provide depth perception
  - Provide variety

**Golf Course Design**
**Safety Considerations**

---

**Routing a Golf Course**

## Golf Course Design
## Safety Considerations

- Adjacent tees and greens should be at least 100 feet apart at their borders
- Adjacent tees and greens should be at least 200 feet apart from their center points
- If space limitations require holes to be located close together, use bunkers, ponds, mounds, and trees to separate the holes

---

## Routing a Golf Course

- Golf holes should be routed clockwise
- Allow right-handed golfers to slice into the course, not out of bounds

**Managing Golf Course Traffic**

---

**Planting a Newly Designed Golf Course**

## Managing Golf Course Traffic

- Allow golf cars only in designated areas
- Limit play
- Post signs, course markers, and barriers
- Rotate cup placement on greens
- Rotate tee markers

---

## Planting a Newly Designed Golf Course

Plant in the following order:

1. Tees and greens
2. Fairways
3. Rough

**Types of Golf Holes**

---

**Golf Course Renovation**

## Types of Golf Holes

- Heroic golf holes require extraordinary maneuvers
- Penal golf holes are not forgiving because they leave little room for error
- Strategic golf holes require thought and consideration

---

## Golf Course Renovation

Reasons to renovate a golf course:
- Change in golf technology
- Change in market demand
- Environmental evolution

# Recreational Golf Experience Phases

## Recreational Golf Experience Phases

1. Anticipation
2. Arrival
3. Participation
4. Cool down
5. Memory

# LEVEL 3

**Merchandising Steps**

---

**Open-to-Buy (OTB) Plan**

## Merchandising Steps

1. Create open-to-buy (OTB) plan
2. Create merchandise assortment plan (MAP)
3. Select vendor
4. Determine price
5. Order and receive merchandise
6. Display and promote merchandise
7. Sell merchandise
8. Monitor sales and inventory levels
9. Make adjustments as needed

---

## Open-to-Buy (OTB) Plan

- Helps a golf professional determine how much money should be spent on merchandise classifications
- Tracks how much money will remain each month to buy or restock inventory
- Maintains inventory levels to support expected future sales
- In an OTB plan, approximately 10% to 25% of all dollars should be uncommitted to allow for flexibility and periodic changes in purchasing

**Establishing an Open-to-Buy (OTB) Plan**

---

**Merchandise Classifications**

## Establishing an Open-to-Buy (OTB) Plan

1. Forecast sales
2. Forecast cost of goods sold
3. Forecast turnover rate
4. Establish beginning-of-month inventory levels
5. Calculate OTB plan budget

---

## Merchandise Classifications

- Examples include men's apparel, women's apparel, shoes, gloves, etc.
- Small golf shops typically have at least 10 merchandise classifications
- Large golf shops have 20 or more merchandise classifications

**Cost of Goods Sold (COGS)**

---

**Cost of Goods Sold**
**as a Percentage of Sales**

## Cost of Goods Sold (COGS)

- Definition: Wholesale price vendors charge for merchandise
- Includes additional costs such as shipping and handling
- Includes merchandise that has been lost or stolen
- COGS $ = beginning of month inventory + purchases – end of month inventory
- COGS % = cost of goods sold in dollars / total retail sales

---

## Cost of Goods Sold as a Percentage of Sales

- Should be between 65% and 75% for hard goods
- Should be between 50% and 60% for soft goods
- "Soft goods" are defined as products consumed in one use

**Inventory Turnover Rate**

---

**Average Turnover Rate Comparison**

## Inventory Turnover Rate

- Definition: Indicates how many times a golf shop's average inventory is sold and reinvested throughout the year
- Turnover rate = total cost of goods sold / average inventory at cost
- The higher a golf shop's inventory turnover rate, the less inventory is needed on hand to reach sales goals
- Highest turnover items are golf balls and shirts
- Excessively high turnover can lead to a higher cost of goods sold percentage
- Poor pricing will result in poor turnover

---

## Average Turnover Rate Comparison

- Average turnover rate for all golf shops is 1.5
- Average turnover rate for private equity PGA facilities is 2.5
- Average turnover rate for all sporting retailers is 3.6
- Average turnover rate for top golf merchandisers is 4.0

Inventory Levels

---

Inventory Tracking Systems

## Inventory Levels

- Average monthly inventory level = annual COGS / turnover rate
- Average inventory at cost = total end of month inventory on hand / length of season
- Inventory levels should increase two months before the peak season begins
- Enough inventory should be on hand at the beginning of the season to cover sales for at least 90 days
- Physical inventory count should be performed at least twice per year

---

## Inventory Tracking Systems

- Financial value inventory tracking indicates the dollar value of inventory on hand and sold, and the history of price changes and markdowns
- Perpetual book inventory tracking indicates changes to merchandise levels, both in terms of dollar value and number of units, on a daily basis or as they occur
- Physical unit inventory tracking indicates the quantity of merchandise on hand, sold, and on order, and the age of the merchandise

**Merchandise Assortment Plan (MAP)**

---

**Establishing a Merchandise Assortment Plan (MAP)**

## Merchandise Assortment Plan (MAP)

- Establishes the sizes, colors, materials, models, styles, brands, price points, and quantities for each product line
- Merchandise should be selected on the basis of:
    - Brand name
    - Compatibility
    - Competition
    - Customer demand
    - Profitability
    - Supply

---

## Establishing a Merchandise Assortment Plan (MAP)

1. Review customer needs
2. Evaluate the previous year's performance by merchandise classification
3. Research market trends
4. Select merchandise to purchase

**Vendor Selection**

---

**Vendor Concentration**

## Vendor Selection

Vendors should be selected on the basis of:

- Advertising support
- Assistance with backroom operations (pricing and tagging)
- Extended billing options
- Product discounts

---

## Vendor Concentration

- Concentrating a golf shop's buying power with few vendors has advantages and disadvantages
- Advantages
  - Faster delivery
  - Individual attention
  - Improved efficiency
  - Quantity discounts
- Disadvantages
  - Fewer sources of information
  - Less access to new trends
  - Possible stock outages

**Planogram**

---

**Extended Billing Strategies**

## Planogram

- Definition: Golf shop floor plan that illustrates where different types of merchandise should be placed
- Departmentalizing a golf shop is part of an effective planogram
- Group merchandise by vendor, size, color, etc.
- Establish "destination areas" in the golf shop that include products customers intend to purchase before entering the shop

---

## Extended Billing Strategies

- Types of extended billing strategies include anticipation dating and spring dating
- Anticipation dating
  - Setting a future date when payment is due
  - Offering a discount for early payment
- Spring dating
  - Golf shop receives merchandise in the fall of the current year, with payment due in April or May of the following year
- Advantages of using extended billing strategies include the opportunity to sell items at no immediate cost, and a reduced number of back orders

**Product Markup Approaches**

---

**Product Markup Examples**

## Product Markup Approaches

- Cost plus markup
- Keystoning
- Manufacturer's suggested retail price
- Mill River Plan

---

## Product Markup Examples

- Cost plus markup: Use a target markup percentage as the basis for pricing merchandise
- Keystoning: Double an item's cost to arrive at the final retail price
- Manufacturer's suggested retail price: Golf shop sets prices according to the manufacturer's suggested retail price
- Mill River Plan: Members pay an initial fee at the beginning of the season and can purchase merchandise at a small percentage above cost

**Markup & Margin Formulas**

---

**Determining Product Markup**

## Markup & Margin Formulas

- Markup $ = retail price – cost
- Markup % = markup $ / cost
- Gross margin $ = retail price – cost
- Gross margin % = markup $ / retail price

---

## Determining Product Markup

- Establish gross margin goals first, then determine what the product markup must be in order to achieve it
- Gross profit margin for a public golf facility should be at least 30%
- Gross profit margin for a private golf facility should be at least 50%
- Actual gross margin will be less than markup because some items will be lost, stolen, or damaged

**Competitive Factors Influencing Markup**

---

**Value Added Factors Influencing Markup**

## Competitive Factors Influencing Markup

- Exclusivity
- Follow the leader
- Opportunistic pricing
- Supply and demand

---

## Value Added Factors Influencing Markup

- Convenience
- Facility image
- Product availability
- Services provided

**Key Performance Indicators**

---

**Gross Margin Return on Investment (GMROI)**

## Key Performance Indicators

- COGS as a % of sales
- Gross margin $
- Gross margin %
- Gross margin return on investment (GMROI)
- Inventory turnover rate
- Revenue per round

---

## Gross Margin Return on Investment (GMROI)

- Calculates the profit made for each dollar spent on inventory
- Measures the true profitability of different products, such as those that have high margins (golf shoes) and those that have high turnover (golf tees)
- Golf shop GMROI between 110% and 160% is excellent
- GMROI = gross margin in dollars / total retail sales

**Merchandise Markdowns**

---

**Temporary vs. Permanent Markdowns**

## Merchandise Markdowns

Merchandise markdowns provide the following benefits:

- Decrease inventory levels
- Increase cash flow
- Remove stale merchandise
- Stimulate sales

---

## Temporary vs. Permanent Markdowns

- Temporary markdown
  - Also referred to as a "point-of-sale" markdown
  - Takes place during special events
- Permanent markdown
  - Permanent reduction in a product's list price
  - Should be indicated on merchandise tags

## Methods of Improving Financial Performance

---

## Consequences of Poor Pricing

## Methods of Improving Financial Performance

- Adjust prices
- Decrease inventory costs
- Increase sales volume

---

## Consequences of Poor Pricing

- Bankruptcy or job loss
- Excess inventory
- Failure to reach financial goals
- Lost sales
- Poor turnover

**Effective Pricing Strategies**

---

**Purchase Order (PO)**

## Effective Pricing Strategies

Effective pricing strategies provide the following benefits:

- Ability to meet overhead costs
- Ability to meet profit goals
- Consistent sales volume

---

## Purchase Order (PO)

Purchase orders identify the following:

- What merchandise is on order
- When merchandise was ordered
- When merchandise will be delivered
- Who ordered merchandise

**Point-of-Sale (POS) System**

---

**Elements of an Attractive Buying Environment**

## Point-of-Sale (POS) System

- Allows for timely reporting of sales information
- Automatically updates a golf shop's open-to-buy (OTB) plan
- Maintains accurate inventory
- Maintains price control

---

## Elements of an Attractive Buying Environment

- Displays
- Fixtures
- Floor layout
- Lighting
- Signage
- Staff selling skills

**Displays & Fixtures**

---

**Sizing Merchandise**

## Displays & Fixtures

- Attention-getting displays
    - Create changing elevations
    - Highlight a coordinated look
    - Make merchandise easily accessible
- Flexible fixtures
    - Enhance the golf shop's image
    - Keep the golf shop looking full when inventory is low
    - Present older merchandise in a new light

---

## Sizing Merchandise

- Hanging merchandise
    - Size items from left to right
    - Begin with the smallest size and increase size as you move to the right
- Folded merchandise
    - Size items from top to bottom
    - Begin with the smallest size and increase size as you move to the bottom

**Maintaining a Golf Shop's Appearance**

---

**Managing a Golf Shop**

## Maintaining a Golf Shop's Appearance

- Daily activities
  - Clean displays and mirrors
  - Organize the counter area
  - Vacuum the floor
- Weekly activities
  - Clean air vents
  - Clean shelves
  - Organize the back room

---

## Managing a Golf Shop

Golf professional should perform the following functions:

1. Track sales performance
2. Analyze variances in sales
3. Adjust factors as needed

**Preparing for a Promotional Event**

---

**Selling Process Steps**

## Preparing for a Promotional Event

1. Set objectives
2. Establish the budget
3. Determine requirements
4. Identify tasks to be completed
5. Schedule activities
6. Communicate the plan to employees

---

## Selling Process Steps

1. Approach the customer
2. Collect key information
3. Present the merchandise
4. Close the sale
5. Build future sales

**Delegating**

---

**Resources / Input / Feedback**

## Delegating

- Definition: Partnership building process that empowers employees
- Not a technique used to control employees
- Manager should consider the capabilities and willingness of an employee before delegating an assignment

---

## Resources / Input / Feedback

- Resources are the basic means available to an employee in completing a task
- Input is the information, circumstances, or events that prompt an employee to take action to complete a task
- Feedback is the specific information an employee receives about the results of his or her actions

**Types of Resources**

---

**Feedback Guidelines**

## Types of Resources

Resources can be:

- Financial
- Human
- Material
- Time-based

---

## Feedback Guidelines

Effective feedback is:

- Based on fair expectations
- Easy to understand
- Objective
- Specific to an employee's actions
- Timely

**Building Blocks of Motivating Work**

---

**Elements of an Effective Work Environment**

## Building Blocks of Motivating Work

Three building blocks of motivating work:

- The performer
- The work assignment
- The work environment

---

## Elements of an Effective Work Environment

- Fair treatment by the manager
- Relevant rules
- Satisfactory work conditions
- Stable work relationship between the manager and employees

## Principles of Motivating Work

---

## 4-Stage Sequence for Correcting Performance Problems

## Principles of Motivating Work

- Autonomy
- Feedback
- Significant work
- Skill variety
- Whole task

---

## 4-Stage Sequence for Correcting Performance Problems

- Stage 1: Joint problem solving with performer
- Stage 2: Reinforced problem solving with performer
- Stage 3: Final decision making with performer
- Stage 4: Termination of employment relationship

**Failure to Correct Performance Problems**

---

**Teaching Philosophy**

## Failure to Correct Performance Problems

Four ways a manager can fail to correct performance problems:

- Failure to involve the employee
- Inaction
- Missed opportunities
- Wrong assumptions

---

## Teaching Philosophy

- Definition: A golf instructor's mission statement
- Summarizes an instructor's views, beliefs, concepts, and attitudes towards the game of golf and how it should be taught
- Instructor must be able to describe and defend each element of his teaching philosophy

**Teaching Approach**

---

**Putting Principles**

## Teaching Approach

- How an instructor communicates with students
- Procedure for executing an instructor's teaching philosophy
- Changes with each student

---

## Putting Principles

- Position eye line over, or slightly inside, the ball
- Square the clubface to the target
- Position the ball forward of center
- Limit body movement
- Use an accelerating stroke

**Putting Grip**

---

**Putter Characteristics**

## Putting Grip

- Select the putting grip that will:
  - Resist wristiness
  - Resist clubface rotation
- Reverse overlap is most common putting grip

---

## Putter Characteristics

- Average length is 35.5 inches
- Average lie is 73.5 degrees
- Average loft is 4.0 degrees
- Average weight is 11.5 ounces

**Grain**

---

**Chipping vs. Pitching**

## Grain

- Bermudagrass has the most grain
- Shiny putting surface means the grain is moving away from the golfer
- Dull putting surface means the grain is moving towards the golfer
- Grain has little effect on a putt's break
- Grain has more effect on the speed of a putt

---

## Chipping vs. Pitching

- Chipping
  - More ground time than air time for the golf ball
  - One-lever stroke (firm wrists)
  - Vertical centerline of the golfer's body should be 2 inches in front of the ball
- Pitching
  - More air time than ground time for the golf ball
  - Two-lever stroke (cocked wrists)
  - Vertical centerline of the golfer's body should be even with the ball
- Transition from chipping to pitching by moving the ball to the centerline of the golfer's body using a wedge

**Principles of Chipping & Pitching**

---

**Practice Shot Routine**

## Principles of Chipping & Pitching

- Grip pressure should be firm or light, but never tight
- Firm grip pressure slows clubhead speed, and light grip pressure increases it
- Feet and hips should be open to restrict the backswing for greater control
- Choke down on the golf club for better control
- Move the ball back in stance if the lie is bare, or to produce a low trajectory ball flight
- Move the ball forward in stance if the lie is fluffy, or to produce a high trajectory ball flight

---

## Practice Shot Routine

1. Survey the lie, terrain, and other external conditions
2. Visualize the shot you want to hit
3. Rehearse the swing until the correct feel is achieved
4. Execute the rehearsed swing
5. Evaluate the shot

## Principles of Hitting a Cut Shot

## Principles of Hitting a Cut-Lob Shot

## Principles of Hitting a Cut Shot

To hit a cut shot:

- Aim the feet and shoulders to the left of the target
- Open the clubface
- Keep the hands and arms back
- Move the body forward

---

## Principles of Hitting a Cut-Lob Shot

To hit a cut-lob shot:

- Move the ball forward in stance
- Open the clubface
- Swing with the arms

**Principles of Hitting a Flop Shot**

---

**Principles of Hitting a Draw**

## Principles of Hitting a Flop Shot

To hit a flop shot:

- Allow the left wrist to break downward
- Strike the ball with a steep descent
- Maintain wristy action through the golf ball

---

## Principles of Hitting a Draw

To hit a draw:

- Sole the clubface square to the target
- Use a closed face grip
- Aim the feet and shoulders to the right of the target

**Uneven Lies**

---

**Sand Wedge Characteristics**

## Uneven Lies

- Sidehill lie with ball above the feet: Tendency is to chunk, pull, or hook the ball
- Sidehill lie with ball below the feet: Tendency is to push, slice, or top the ball
- Uphill lie: Tendency is to chunk, pull, or hit behind the ball
- Downhill lie: Tendency is to top, push, or hit behind the ball

---

## Sand Wedge Characteristics

- To easily remove the ball from a greenside bunker, a sand wedge has:
  - Breadth
  - Camber
  - Sole inversion
- Gene Sarazan is credited with inventing the modern sand wedge

**Breadth & Camber**

**Greenside Bunker Shot**

## Breadth & Camber

- Breadth is the width of a golf club's sole
- Camber is the curvature of a golf club's sole
- Camber helps irons move smoothly across the turf and dig less into the ground when taking divots

---

## Greenside Bunker Shot

- Play the ball 4 to 6 inches left of the golfer's vertical centerline
- Bounce is promoted if the heel of the golf club leads
- Dig is promoted if the toe of the golf club leads
- "V" shaped swing will produce a higher, softer shot
- "U" shaped swing will produce a lower, longer shot

**Controlling Distance on Bunker Shots**

---

**Buried Greenside Bunker Shot**

## Controlling Distance on Bunker Shots

Distance is controlled by:

- Angle of approach
- Blade position
- Length of backswing
- Length of follow through
- Pace of backswing
- Volume of sand

---

## Buried Greenside Bunker Shot

To hit a buried greenside bunker shot:

- Play the ball back in stance to increase penetration with the clubface
- Turn the toe of clubhead in for a knife-like leading edge to easily penetrate through the sand

**Fairway Bunker Shot**

---

**Wind Conditions**

## Fairway Bunker Shot

- Contact the ball first when hitting from a fairway bunker
- Choke down on the club as far down as the golfer's feet are buried in the sand
- Firm sand requires less bounce
- Soft sand requires more bounce

---

## Wind Conditions

- Wind against the golfer
  - Choose a stronger club
  - Choke down on the club for better control
  - Move the ball back in stance
  - Shorten the swing
- Downwind
  - Tee the ball higher
  - Do not over swing
- Side wind
  - Let the ball ride the wind for maximum distance
  - Do not fight the wind

**Body Types**

---

**Endomorph**

## Body Types

3 basic human body types:

- Endomorph
- Ectomorph
- Mesomorph

---

## Endomorph

- Endomorph is characterized by:
  - Low muscle tone
  - Small bones
  - Soft, round frame
- Endomorphs are generally poor athletes

**Ectomorph**

---

**Mesomorph**

## Ectomorph

- Ectomorph is characterized by:
  - Long arms and legs
  - Short trunk
  - Thin bones
  - Thin muscles
- Ectomorphs generally have high endurance levels

---

## Mesomorph

- Mesomorph is characterized by:
  - Big bones
  - Broad shoulders
  - Large muscles
  - Slender waist
- Mesomorphs generally have increased strength

**Senior Golfers**

---

**Group Lessons**

## Senior Golfers

- Need to adopt a more clockwise-positioned grip to reduce forearm and hand rotation
- Senior golfers typically experience:
    - Decreased strength
    - Decreased range of motion

---

## Group Lessons

- Semi-private teaching lesson includes 2 to 4 students
- Group lesson should be limited to 5 to 12 students in total, allowing 3 to 5 minutes each for individual instruction

**Golf Clinics**

---

**Teaching Left-Handed Golfers**

## Golf Clinics

- Participation clinic includes a blend of demonstration, observation, and coaching students while they hit golf balls
- Demonstration clinic educates and entertains students by blending fun with fundamentals

---

## Teaching Left-Handed Golfers

- Right-handed golf instructor should use himself as a mirror image to teach swing fundamentals to a left-handed student
- Although 10% to 15% of Americans are left-handed, only 3% to 6% play golf left-handed

**Factors Affecting a Golfer's Skill Level**

---

**Types of Golf Facilities**

## Factors Affecting a Golfer's Skill Level

- Cardiovascular endurance
- Flexibility
- Muscular endurance
- Strength

---

## Types of Golf Facilities

- Public
- Private
- Semi-private

**Types of Private Golf Facilities**

---

**Equity Golf Facility**

## Types of Private Golf Facilities

- Developer-owned
- Equity
- Privately managed

---

## Equity Golf Facility

- Type of private golf facility
- Owned by the golf club's members
- Service, not profit, is the operational goal

**Privately Managed Golf Facility**

---

**Food & Beverage Operation**

## Privately Managed Golf Facility

- Type of private golf facility
- Goals include:
    - High profit
    - Full membership

---

## Food & Beverage Operation

- Primary goal is to achieve total customer satisfaction
- At least 50% of a golf facility's non-dues related income should come from the food and beverage operation
- Largest expense in a typical food and beverage operation is payroll, followed by supplies

**Food & Beverage Inventory Control**

---

**P-A-C-E**

## Food & Beverage Inventory Control

- "Par stock" refers to the predetermined quantities of food items the Food and Beverage Director wants to have on hand at all times
- Food and beverage purchasing is generally based on the bid system

---

## P-A-C-E

- Successful food and beverage operations follow the acronym P-A-C-E
- P-A-C-E stands for:
    - Primary plan
    - Alternative plan
    - Contingency plan
    - Emergency plan

**Food Cost Control**

---

**Picture Board**

## Food Cost Control

- Definition: Following the golf facility's predetermined standards, while exercising restraint over the price the facility pays to purchase, prepare, and sell food
- Applies to the following areas:
    - Menu
    - Purchasing
    - Receiving
    - Service
    - Storeroom

---

## Picture Board

- Demonstrates the standard plate presentation
- Should be maintained in the kitchen
- Maintains consistency for the food and beverage operation

**Menu**

---

**Menu Development Steps**

## Menu

- Menu is the most basic and important control tool used in a food and beverage operation
- To determine a menu item's base selling price, multiply the entrée cost by the price multiplier
- Price multiplier is equal to 100% divided by the food cost goal
- Menu item's standard portion cost = total cost of recipe / number of portions

---

## Menu Development Steps

1. Develop the menu concept
2. Develop recipes
3. Test recipes
4. Determine menu costs
5. Print the menu
6. Train staff

**Standard Recipe**

---

**Elements of a Standard Recipe**

## Standard Recipe

- Definition: Blueprint used to develop a food and beverage menu item
- Benefits of using a standard recipe:
    - Less supervision required
    - Product consistency
    - Standard portion cost
    - Standard portion size

---

## Elements of a Standard Recipe

- Ingredients
- Quantities
- Preparation procedure
- Portion size
- Garnish

**Levels of Food & Beverage Service**

---

**Food & Beverage Staffing Levels**

## Levels of Food & Beverage Service

Six levels of food and beverage service in the golf industry:

- Banquets
- Carryout
- Formal fine dining
- Full service
- Off-site catering
- On-course concessions

---

## Food & Beverage Staffing Levels

- Carryout service
  - 1 attendant per 20 to 30 rounds of golf per hour
- Formal fine dining
  - 1 cook per 10 customers
  - 1 dishwasher per 2 servers and cooks
  - 1 front server per 12 customers
  - 1 maitre d' per 4 front servers

**Food & Beverage Staffing Levels**

---

**Stages of the Hiring Process**

## Food & Beverage Staffing Levels

- Full service
  - 1 bartender / busser / host / washer per 5 to 6 servers
  - 1 cook and server per 12 customers per hour
- Off-site catering
  - 1 bartender per 100 customers
  - 1 server per 2 tables for plated meals
  - 1 server per 3 tables for a buffet
  - 1 server per 30 customers for a reception
- On-course concessions
  - 1 attendant per 50 to 60 rounds of golf

---

## Stages of the Hiring Process

1. Recruiting
2. Interviewing
3. Hiring
4. Orientation

**Staff Orientation**

---

**Methods Used to Retain Staff**

## Staff Orientation

- Answer employee questions
- Explain employee benefits
- Explain pay periods
- Review policies and procedures
- Tour the facility

---

## Methods Used to Retain Staff

- Offer advancement opportunities
- Provide adequate compensation
- Provide thorough training

**Characteristics of a Well-Maintained Storeroom**

---

**Dram Shop Laws**

## Characteristics of a Well-Maintained Storeroom

- A well-maintained storeroom has carefully regulated:
    - Air circulation
    - Humidity
    - Sanitation
    - Temperature
- A well-maintained storeroom uses the FIFO (first-in-first-out) inventory management method

---

## Dram Shop Laws

- Holds liquor-serving establishments liable for the actions of their customers
- Encourages restaurant and bar operators to use sound judgment when serving liquor

Liquor Service Policies

---

Failing to Comply With
Food & Beverage Regulations

## Liquor Service Policies

- Liquor license must be obtained before offering liquor for sale
- Liquor license must be displayed at all times
- Liquor-serving establishments must purchase liquor from a licensed vendor

---

## Failing to Comply With Food & Beverage Regulations

Possible penalties for failing to comply with food and beverage regulations:

- Closing the food and beverage operation
- Lawsuit
- Loss of license, permit, or certificate
- Monetary fine

# ABOUT THE AUTHORS

Ryan Brandeburg is a PGA member and serves as the Director of Golf for The Lodge at Kauri Cliffs and The Farm at Cape Kidnappers on the North Island of New Zealand. Both golf courses consistently rank among the top 50 in the world, and Ryan's responsibilities include managing the daily operations and strategic direction for each course. Ryan has an extensive background in private and resort operations, and has formerly served as the Acting Director of Golf at Waldorf Astoria Golf Club in Orlando, Florida, and the Head Golf Professional at Naples Grande Golf Club in Naples, Florida. In addition, Ryan is a contributing columnist to international golf publications including Golf Digest Korea and Golf Travel China.

Matthew Brandeburg is a Certified Financial Planner and President of Bridgeway Financial Group, LLC in Columbus, Ohio. Matthew is the author of the books "Financial Planning For Your First Job", "Your Guide to the CFP Certification Exam", "CFP Certification Exam Practice Question Workbook", "CFP Certification Exam Flashcard Review Books", "Professional Golf Management (PGM) Practice Question Workbook", and "Professional Golf Management (PGM) Interactive Flashcard Book". He is also the creator of the mobile apps "Investment Allocator" and "Pocket Financial Planner". In addition, Matthew teaches the class "Financial Planning in your 20s and 30s" at Ohio State University.

# INDEX

## C

**G**

**M**

**N**



**O**

**S**

**U**



**V**



**W - Z**

14042252R00187

Made in the USA
Charleston, SC
17 August 2012